Shaken Baby Syndrome: an exploration of alternative explanation

Author: Lynne D M Noble

All rights reserved. No part of this publication may be reproduced, stored in a retrieval system or transmitted in any form or by any means, without prior permission in writing of the author Lynne D M Noble, or as expressly agreed by law, or under terms agreed with the appropriate reprographics right organisation.

You must not circulate this book in any other binding or cover and you must impose the same condition on any acquirer.

Independently published 2024

About the Author

Lynne Noble was born in 1953 in Huddersfield, West Yorkshire. From a very early age, Lynne showed an interest in nutrition and genetics avidly reading any books that she could get her hands on at the time.

Initially, Lynne studied orthopaedics but events led her to work with the elderly mentally infirm. Here, her interest in neurodegenerative disorders and pain syndromes developed.

Lynne undertook rigorous programmes of study, completing her Cert Ed., (FE) BSc (Hons) and Adv. Dip Education simultaneously before moving onto her M.Ed.

From there she took further demanding programmes in Human Nutrition, Pharmacology, Neuroscience, Genetics and Immunology. During this time, she was given many prestigious awards for her academic work. It was noted then that Lynne was not afraid of tackling difficult subjects.

She began her law degree but ill health prevented her from pursuing this. However, in this time, she moved from being a foster parent to adoptive parent.

She has been instrumental in setting up projects in the community for disadvantaged groups.

She is a member of the Guild of Health Writers.

Now retired, she lives with her husband in a historic Georgian riverside town in the West Midlands. She enjoys gardening, watching her husband bowling and researching.

Author Lynne Noble at home

Preface

This is a true story about a case of Shaken Baby Syndrome that never was but it mirrors many of the events that took place in the early 2000's.

In reading this account, you are asked to put all prior thoughts, all feelings of revulsion that you might feel and look at the evidence logically leaving all emotion aside. This is the only way that the evidence placed before you will be done any justice.

In the early 2000's due to the growing numbers of alleged Shaken Baby Syndrome cases coming before the courts an MP – John Hemming – became involved in looking at what happening when so many were protesting their innocence.

There is little to be found of what he achieved. Any reference to his involvement with looking at cases involving alleged Shaken Baby Syndrome are not longer to be found on the internet. However, due to my involvement with a case, I had cause to ring up his office to make enquiries about alleged discrepancies in the case I was looking at.

I was met with an extremely churlish response along the lines of 'no one can prove that they didn't harm their baby.'

It did not seem to me that anyone was really looking at the case independently but that such support groups set up were merely containing a group of people with a genuine grievance.

Most of the families involved were from impoverished backgrounds. Poverty does not make a bad parent, more of a resourceful one. I have come across bad parenting in those who do not have to count their pennies in order to get to the end of the week. Still labels stick.

One of the injustices caused was that alleged 'baby batterers' did not have the funds to fight their case and so were reliant on social services to provide and fund the solicitor.

It was, of course, social services who were more likely than not, taking the poor, confused and generally innocent parents to court.

Solicitors who were hired and paid for by social services were hardly likely to be independent.

Much is said and done but it is hardly the truth. For example, I have heard one solicitor state that if robust evidence is provided for appeal then we will take it forward.

In one case, robust evidence was provided and sent with due diligence to the said solicitor. It was ignored in spite of follow up requests to take the case to appeal.

Note well that I am not saying that babies or children are never abused; they are but not on the scale that came to light at the turn of the century.

This book attempts to bring one true story to you of the practices that were in place a couple of decades ago.

Even when evidence, which proved that what prosecuting council was stating, could not be true, it was hidden for judges, as I found out, have the right to decide what evidence is heard or not; something that I find shocking.

The social worker who hunted for evidence in the accused's file, chose carefully citing the birth mother - who was known to have abused the accused as a child - as harming himself.

A report from a Consultant Paediatrician was left in the file. It stated, that 'no child could whip themselves on their own back and leave the marks that were left there.'

Still the courts chose to believe the birth mother of the Defendant and it was used to prove that he had a 'personality disorder' and would therefore automatically go on to harm his own son.

My eyes roll at this. Are we really making payment to alleged professionals to make such trite and untrue statements?

None of the evidence ever proved that the Defendant harmed his own son but where the prosecution did not have the evidence, it made it up and it was accepted. The expert witnesses were complicit too.

Where the Defendant obtained robust evidence, it was ignored. I watched a theatre, not the just, reflective and wise institution that had been my belief.

All the while, a young man, who loved his first born dearly, sat bewildered and mute, in the proceedings, at what was going on, barely able to comprehend what was happening.

Just prior to the trial I was asked to help look at the evidence and I went through hundreds of pages of documentary evidence in one night. Nothing added up. It was a legal simulation designed to give the appearance of achieving justice for a deed that evidence proved could not have been an act of the Defendant.

Was there a more insidious cause of the multiplicity of Shaken Baby Syndrome cases that came together so long ago? Something that the authorities did not want to get out? Could this case be included among those?

Let's look at this one case to begin with, follow it through, reflect on the anomalies and follow this up with some robust research that has been kept hidden since those times.

For ease of clarity, Lawrence is the young man accused of harming his own child. He was placed in care as a young boy after being the subject of abuse himself.

The story alternates between Lawrence as a young child coming into foster care with Carly and his experiences as an adult. Nothing is made up although names have been changed to protect those involved in the events written about.

Please suspend any opinions that you hold that those abused must automatically go onto abuse their own children. It has not been my experience of the very long line of children coming into my care who had difficult starts. It made them even more determined not to repeat the mistakes of their caregivers at the time.

At times I may add comments and these will be italicised for ease of understanding.

The beginning of it all

April 2009

Carly had read the letter for the third time before making a decision. She hadn't heard from Lawrence for a few years now, nor had she expected to. There was a pattern you see. She could see It now but it had had to happen a few times before she knew it was a pattern.

June 1991

She had met Lawrence when he was a five-year old. He had stood defiantly in the kitchen, his clenched fists hiding the grubby fingernails, pretending that he wasn't in the least bit interested in what she was doing. Only he was. Every now and again he would glance at Carly, only to drop his eyes almost immediately.

His body was tense, like a coiled up spring – ready for fight or flight. Rebelliousness was woven into every sinew and muscle of his body. His hands clawed. Carly wondered what he was thinking that could had been converted into such an action – the outward show of inner turmoil.

Carly busied herself with the cups. She knew that he was watching her open the bottle of orange juice.

'Would you like a drink?' she enquired.

He didn't answer so she passed him some orange in a plastic cup.

He drank it noisily and thirstily. This was not surprising considering that the social worker had been alerted to Lawrence's plight by the headmistress. She had reported that Lawrence had arrived at school with only a small cube of cheese to sustain him for the whole day.

She had also been concerned about the ingrained dirt in Lawrence's fingers and knees, the unsuitable clothing he was wearing which didn't look as though it had been washed for many days. Mostly, though, she was concerned about Lawrence's hunger and his behaviour.

'When you've finished you can put your cup in the sink if you like.' Carly hadn't seen Lawrence creep away. He was crouched down in the corner, like a trapped animal, waiting, waiting………

As Carly finished speaking, he uncurled his battered body and hurled the cup towards the sink. It rolled and clattered creating sprays of tiny droplets as it bounced around in the sink.

Lawrence had crouched around waiting for the next move.

Carly sucked the air between her teeth. This was going to be a long six weeks – that was for sure.

Only, as she found out later, it wasn't just for six weeks that she would be looking after this little boy, although she could honestly say that these were the longest six weeks that she had ever had to endure. Six weeks that she would not want to repeat ever again; she and Lawrence had survived it but, only just.

The damage Lawrence had sustained ran deep but there was a resilience within him, a hope, a determination and his eyes were quick and intelligent.

In the end, he stayed all his childhood, blossoming into a captivating and loveable child.

In all respects he had a golden future to look forward to.

The Letter; April 2009

Carly picked up the letter again. It read,

Dear Mum,

I am sorry that it such a long time since I have been in touch. I am living in London now. I have a girlfriend, Jenna and a little boy called Anthony. I was hoping we could meet up. There is something that I need to tell you.

Love

Lawrence

That was all it said. It had been written on the sort of paper that you would normally pull out of a school exercise book. Still it had been written in Lawrence's best handwriting. It included his address and telephone number.

Carly had kept the news of the letter hidden from Mike, her husband. She needed to chew things over, consider options. She had always been a fairly cautious character but that generally had stood her in good stead.

She was in the process of moving. Her life had never been easy. Indeed, she could not recall one day when it had been.

The trigger to move had arisen when one of her pupil's mother had casually stated that she would be moving about a mile away. She was tired of this community and its problems, the young mum had divulged. She could remember when it was a coherent community – when people looked after each other and took pride in where they lived. The young mum had pulled a face before muttering 'It's not like that anymore.'

That conversation had been the impetus to move for Carly, who had never really settled in Ashbury. Mike had quickly agreed; finding somewhere suitable was a different matter though. It had taken them a year before they found a bungalow on the edge of the countryside in a village which took pride in its appearance, where there was little traffic and the neighbours were actually civil.

Carly didn't want her retirement to be spoiled. She folded Lawrence's letter up and dropped it into the bin. There were only a few boxes left to pack now. They were moving tomorrow. She would not be sorry to be leaving this place.

Most of the boxes had already been taken across to her new home. The former owner had allowed Carly to stash some of the items they were less likely to need in the garage. Carly had spent a great deal of time disposing of unwanted items at her favourite charity shop. She was, after all, moving from a four- bedroom home to a two bedded bungalow.

She did not realise that the whole process of moving could be so difficult. What should she keep? Was there room for nostalgia – for keeping all the birthday cards which had been so lovingly made by all the children who had passed through her hands.

'Shall we take these over now?' Mike had walked in wiping the oil off his hand with an old cloth. 'It'll make things easier tomorrow, I think!'

Carly nodded. She didn't want to be here, anyway. She had already left Ashbury mentally. She had done so on the day that they identified the bungalow as being their forever home.

Mike picked up the first box, with practised ease, and strode off to the car. Carly bent down and dipped her hand into the waste bin. She fished the letter out deftly and pushed it firmly into her pocket. She would ponder the foolishness of this action, later.

June 1991; the first day

When Carly had undressed Lawrence that first night, she had noticed huge bruises overlying Lawrence's tawny skin. She had never seen bruises like them before. Some were as big as her fist.

Strangely, Lawrence did not appear to notice them nor did they appear to cause him pain. He was intent on having a fight with his pyjamas, protesting loudly that he did not want to go to bed. Now and again he would pick up his toothpaste and smear it on his toothbrush with great generosity. The he would open his mouth and bare his teeth in an exaggerated grin. Flecks of toothpaste would fly in all directions while Lawrence scrubbed away, oblivious to everything around him.

Carly was glad that she had managed to get this far with Lawrence. He had screamed solidly for two hours after she had told him it was time for bed. The other two fostered children had looked on in consternation while Carly's youngest son had silently stuffed cotton wool in his ears before going to make himself a sandwich.

It was clear that Lawrence did not understand about bedtimes or indeed any other structures in households which came under the general heading of 'rules.' Really, rules just made life a little easier. People knew what to expect when there were rules. Lawrence had either not come across them before or did not think that they applied to him.

On the way upstairs he had opened his mouth so wide that Carly, for a moment, thought he might swallow his head. At the same time that he started yelling, Lawrence grabbed onto the stair rails. As fast as Carly prised open his other hand had grasped the bannister rail. Carly was normally fit but she could feel herself puffing and panting with the exertion of it all.

The other boys thought that this was great fun. They bobbed their heads around the doorway smiling at all the commotion. Carly was not sure it was a laughing matter but she was grateful that the rest of the family were not alarmed by the unexpected outburst.

The two other foster children were going to new forever homes tomorrow. They had arrived within days of each other, six months ago, and had gelled instantly. They were happy and good natured and had been no trouble. Carly had grown to love them dearly but they were now going to move to different forever homes. She would miss them greatly. Yes, she would miss them more than she was prepared to admit to.

30th April 2009

It had taken Carly and Mike most of the day to move in and find new homes for all the items that they had brought with them. Carly had pared down her possessions admirably, but there were still many pieces of furniture for which there wasn't any room in the bungalow. She had misjudged the amount of room available. Of course, it had looked huge when it was empty; It would, wouldn't it?

'I have some news to tell you.' Carly withdrew the letter from her pocket. 'This came from Lawrence.' She held it out towards Mike who took it slowly before reading it. His face was expressionless.

'What do you intend to do?'

'I don't know. I was going to ignore it but now I'm not sure. It's strange hearing from him after all these years. I might answer it. He doesn't know where we live, anyway. I suppose we could find out what the news is.'

Mike nodded. At least he did not attempt to sway Carly either way. In the end it would be her decision and he would support her.

The second day June 1991

The social worker had popped in the following day. It was only a brief visit to say that she would be setting up contact with a man who Lawrence saw as his real dad although in truth he wasn't. This was followed up by the social worker's description of Lawrence putting his hands over her eyes, when she was driving, in a game of hide and seek.

Carly smiled inwardly, she could just see it happening. Outwardly, she nodded sympathetically, Really, such behaviour could have had tragic consequences.

A date and time was fixed for Carly to meet the Smiths. The Smith family consisted of Paul Smith, who, although not Lawrence's birth father, did not want him to know any different. Paul Smith lived with his parents. His father was dying from cancer but was still determined to visit. Anyway, someone had to accompany Paul Smith when he saw Lawrence for it was he, social services had decided, who had been responsible for Lawrence's extensive bruising.

01/05/2009

Carly posted the letter the following day. Even after making her final decision she had been hesitant. She had not placed her new address or telephone number in the letter. She knew the local café owner well and he was happy to allow Carly to use his address to receive post.

Carly did not expect to hear anything for a while but, almost by return of post, a huge envelope was delivered to the café. When she opened it out tumbled a number of photographs and a very newsy letter. She did not immediately pick up the letter. She picked up each photo and inspected it, scrutinising every little detail. Lawrence looked the way that she expected him to look now that he was a grown man. He hadn't changed in spite of all the years but now he was standing proudly with babe in arms. There was no doubting who the father was, Anthony looked just like Lawrence.

A further photo showed Lawrence standing with a young lady with the same brown eyes and skin that he had. Carly assumed that was Jenna. She was pretty and young and alive.

Carly sincerely hoped that if Lawrence had not married her already that the news would be that he intended doing so.

The café owner was watching Carly intently. She showed him the photos but slipped the letter back into the envelope. She would read it later when no-one was around.

Carly took to the Smith's instantly. Paul Smith was a huge man with folds of tawny skin overlapping the edges of his clothing. A small mop of wavy jet black hair perched precariously on top of his head as though it wasn't his own but had been an unwise purchase for which he was determined to get his money's worth.

His father was a diminutive man, sans hair – no doubt as a result of chemotherapy – who made up for his lack of size through his vibrant personality. 'Nothing', he kept informing Carly, 'was good enough for his Lawrence. Lawrence had been badly treated, they had been badly treated. They loved Lawrence and wouldn't hurt him'

Their sincerity was tangible. Carly felt an instant bond for this family whose love for Lawrence was clear. She could not imagine that they would have inflicted those bruises either. They were aggrieved by events and wanted justice but most of all they wanted their Lawrence to be happy. Carly promised that she would do what she could.

It was clear anyway, that the Smiths were unlikely to have been responsible for Lawrence's injuries. As soon as Lawrence had seen them arrive, he had flown down the road, to the car and had buried himself in his 'dad's' flesh. No abused child would have done that.

The social worker had arranged for Lawrence to return to school. This was some distance away and Carly did not drive. Given Lawrence's tendency to play hide and seek with the driver of the car by placing his hands over the driver's eyes, it was decided that a taxi, complete with carer, would arrive to take him to school every day and bring him home afterwards. As Carly found out, that wasn't the difficult bit. The difficult bit was getting Lawrence dressed to go to school. He did not want to go to school.

Lawrence for all that he was only five was a very wiry and determined chap. As fast as Carly managed to get a sock on him, he managed to pull it off. The battles did not get any easier and they often left Carly exhausted.

Lawrence was bright though. One the first night that he had spent at Carly's house, he had got up the following morning and pronounced that, as he was so bored, he had counted up to a thousand in threes. He had stared at Carly defiantly, daring her to argue with him. Indeed, he was ready for an argument. His fists had balled up at his side, his knuckles white with the effort.

'Go on then!' Carly had challenged him.

With a childlike chant, Lawrence counted quickly and confidently in threes for a number of minutes until Carly had laughed and said she could see that he was indeed very bright.

Lawrence had seemed pleased with this but quickly resumed his combative pose.

It seemed that Lawrence would not have difficulties with school work. He could already read and write. This had been demonstrated by Lawrence writing every known swear word on the paving slabs just outside the garden. What had struck Carly was that they were all spelt correctly.

05/05/2009

Carly fingered the letter again. It did not say much over what Lawrence had already said. He was in trouble but it did not say what sort of trouble. The photos did not seem to confirm that. They were evidence of a lovely closely knit and happy family. This was something that Carly had always wanted for Lawrence since his own birth family had been such a fractured one.

It was not like Lawrence to ask for help though. He had remained an independent little chap as he blossomed in Carly's care. He was resilient and adept and he did not need much help to do anything since he was more than capable himself, anyway.

Of course, there had been many 'heart in the mouth' moments with Lawrence. Not wanting to go to the toilet he had pee'd into the wardrobe.

When smoke had started rising from the socket at the back, he had screamed like a banshee.

He had climbed up the tallest tree he could find and edged along the branch until It began to bend under his weight. Carly had only gone to the toilet for a couple of minutes. It took some heart stopping minutes to coax Lawrence down from the tree.

On another day he had been playing in the loft and cartwheeled across the floor tumbling down the full length of the loft ladders at the end.

On another occasion, she found him standing in the garden fish pond with a nonchalant expression on his face. And then, of course how could she forget those occasions when he had broken his arm. Yes, how could she forget those.

Yet, Lawrence had never asked for help before. That was the deciding factor.

'Mike! I think it's time to go down to London to see Lawrence.'

By the end of the day the arrangements were made to see Lawrence, Anthony and Jenna, the following week.

Mid June 1991

The telephone was insistent in its ringing. Carly wasn't sure whether she would pick it up. Her hand was covered in pastry. Nevertheless, she walked ungraciously to the telephone and picked it up.

A disembodied voice said, 'This is Lawrence's headmistress. Can you come and pick Lawrence up? We're excluding him for the day....'

'Excluding Lawrence! Why?'

'He did a cartwheel in the corridor.'

'Did he hurt anybody?'

'No, but that's not the point.'

What is the point then?'

'He did a cartwheel in the corridor'.

'You're excluding him for being happy?'

The telephone went dead. Silence hung between incredulity and anger.

Mid May 2009

Carly did not find the journey down to London agreeable. She was a country girl at heart. Miles of motorway depressed her spirits. She did not like the speed or the noise or the crowded motorway cafes which resembled Ashbury – jaded and unloved. The stench of the fumes filled her nostrils and made her wrinkle her nose.

Mike was used to this. He had worked in London. He knew the route like the back of his hand. Carly hoped that Lawrence would appreciate the sacrifice that she had made. This was out of her comfort home. She had lived in one town all her life and rarely ventured forth.

She had been down to London before when she had first met Mike and he was keen to introduce her to his friends. She had gone with good grace but she was grateful when they had returned home. In time, the peace and quiet of the country had wound itself into Mike's soul. She knew it would eventually.

They had arranged to meet Lawrence near some offices. Everything seemed to be offices by the time they had reached the Smoke. It was big, impersonal, confusing.

She was glad that Mike was at home in this environment.

She scanned the street where they were to meet Lawrence. She did not expect him to be late. She had brought him up with some manners and she did not think that would have changed except now he was 25 years old and the last time she had seen him was when he was fifteen.

'There he is!' Mike shouted in triumph.

Yes, there he was, only now Lawrence had grown to well over six feet tall but he still had that broad and ready smile as he waved them into the side of the road. He looked relaxed and confident – certainly not the demeanour of someone who had stated that he was in trouble.

Mid June 1991

It was a two mile walk to pick up Lawrence. The school was not on a direct bus route and, as the crow flies, it was far quicker to walk across the fields and the local churchyard and through the winding narrow streets of the next village before finding the school nestled again a hillside, almost hidden from the hustle and bustle of nearby village life.

The school doors were heavy. They gave a little and opened into a corridor. It was quiet – more like a morgue than a school. Carly could not find anything that would direct her to the head teacher's office. She hovered in between confusion and uncertainty before making a decision about which route to take. It was the right one.

The head teacher was an imposing figure with an accusatory air. She wanted Carly to know that Lawrence was disruptive and aggressive and how dare he do a cartwheel in the corridor. If Carly had not been made of sterner stuff she might have found this woman more than a little intimidating. As it was, life had toughened her up. She waited until the head teacher had vented her spleen before being led to Lawrence's classroom.

There was a lot going on. Lawrence was sitting at a table with some other children who were learning to count to ten. Carly was incredulous. Lawrence could count up to one thousand in threes. Why hadn't they picked up o that? She could see why Lawrence could be disruptive. He must be very, very bored. She could see the tension in his body. He was hyper-vigilant, surveying the classroom and the other children, constantly.

Lawrence seemed pleased to see Carly. He wouldn't hold her hand. He did not like contact unless it was with Paul Smith who he appeared to love dearly. Instead, Lawrence followed Carly out trailing about one metre after her. There was some sense of belonging but, in a way, it was a reluctant belonging.

The two-mile journey back home did nothing to curb Lawrence's energy. He was sporting more bruising now. Maybe he'd had a fight or something. Carly did not ask. He seemed pleased, yet confused at being sent home for doing a cartwheel. Carly could understand his confusion. He had been happy – probably for one of only a handful of times in his life – and he had been punished over the top, for it.

The following day a planned meeting was to take place at the school with the head teacher, Carly and the social worker. It was not a happy meeting. The head teacher had nothing good to say about Lawrence. She was strident in her opinions about Lawrence and his disruptive behaviour. The social worker seemed cowed by her.

Carly ventured, 'Perhaps he is bored. He is very intelligent.'

'Bored!' the head teacher thundered. 'Intelligent! Just look where he's come from.'

Lawrence was still capable of giving huge bear hugs. Why not? Carly had taught him how to hug when he had been with her for just a few weeks. He still had his easy manner and coiled up energy. He had grown up to be a fine young man.

'Let's find somewhere for coffee,' he suggested, pointing Carly and Mike down the busy, crowded street. 'I want you to meet Jenna, today. She's going to put you up and she just wants to make sure that the house is ready for you.' Lawrence smiled. It was clear that she meant a great deal to him.

'What about Anthony? When will we meet Anthony?' Carly asked.

The smile slipped a little from Lawrence's face. 'Anthony's in care, Mum. That's what I wanted to see you about.'

Carly swilled the dregs of the tea around in her cup. She needed time to process that information. It was the last thing she had expected.

'In care?' she repeated after a few seconds. 'Why, Lawrence, why?'

Lawrence was pleased that he had learned how to tie his shoelaces, make scrambled egg as well as toast. He soaked up anything that he was taught. It was just as well as he was often excluded for the smallest of things. The last time he had been excluded was because an apology that he offered a classmate was not loud enough.

Carly had clarified that he had, indeed, apologised for a minor misdemeanour but the dinner lady had wanted a louder apology. When Lawrence had refused – which Carly entirely agreed with – because he had already done so, he was excluded. At least, Carly consoled herself with, he was learning something at home which is more than he was doing at school.

He had already outstayed the six weeks that the social worker had said he would be staying with Carly. He was still full of energy and very wary but he was blossoming into a delightful little boy who wanted to know everything about what was going on.

Carly seemed to be more and more involved in planning meetings but, one thing was for sure, Lawrence would be with here over the six weeks' summer holidays. At that stage the social worker had arranged for Carly to spend a couple of weeks helping to run a children's camp to which Lawrence, and Carly's youngest birth son, would also attend.

Lawrence had never slept in a tent before nor run in a field full of sheep and streams and long grass. His slim brown legs raced around the field, jumped over streams, flew over stiles and all the time, Carly watched a confident and happy little boy emerge from whatever nightmare he had been cocooned in, in the past.

Sometimes, Lawrence would take Carly's hand but it was only brief. He wanted to be off. The canteen was much more exciting. It contained beef burgers and sausages and chocolate biscuits and Lawrence wanted to try them all and, in larger quantities than most.

There was barely a thin sheet of darkness between day and morning at the height of summer. Lawrence slept when the light faded and arose when the sun poked her head up across the far field. He, as always, was delighted when he found that the sheep had wandered into the field and were nibbling the grass around the tent.

He was impatient when the campers did not get up at the break of day. He found a large pan and lid and called them to breakfast at 5am. He got away with it. He was five and cute and no-one, just no-one wanted to wipe the smile off his face.

Half way through the week when the corn was golden and the grasshoppers 'zizz zizzed' as they rubbed their legs together, the camp leader decided that they would take a short walk into town. Lawrence was captivated by the butterflies cavorting over the wayside. He carried a slender stick and sometimes he would poke it into the dry stone walling at the side of the road to see if anything would tumble out. Nothing did but it didn't stop him trying.

The road became more treacherous. There had clearly been a number of horses which had relieved themselves on this patch. Lawrence wrinkled his nose up but continued investigating everything that came his way.

Round a bend, it was clear why the road had been splattered with manure for a small stables lay nestled under overhanging trees. Lawrence stopped and stared at the groom who was striding across the courtyard with a whip in his hand.

Almost imperceptibly he whispered, 'My mum used to hit me with a whip like that only the one she used, was bigger than that one.' Then he carried on as though what he had conveyed was of little consequence.

Mid May 2009

'I've been arrested and charged, Mum, with causing Anthony harm.' Lawrence's brave demeanour had slipped now. Some of the little boy that Carly remembered had seeped out from the tall, young and confident young man that Lawrence had become.

Carly knew better than to ask if he had. He wasn't capable of hurting anyone. Lawrence had always been energetic and enquiring but he certainly wasn't abusive.

'What happened?'

'Anthony was staying with me...'

'Staying with you? Are you and Jenna not together?'

Lawrence looked uncomfortable. He shuffled awkwardly on his chair. 'We are together but I live in a different part of London.'

'That doesn't sound like being together to me, Lawrence.'

'I have a flat. It's only small. Jenna had to go out somewhere so I looked after Anthony. I had to go to the toilet. It's a communal toilet down the corridor. I couldn't take Anthony so I left him on the bed. I thought he'd be OK until I got back.'

Carly nodded encouragingly while Mike continued sipping his tea, in silence.

'When I got back, Anthony had fallen off the bed. He was lying between the bed and the little bedside cabinet, roaring his head off. I gave him some milk and he calmed down, he had some red marks around his eyes but that was all.'

Jenna picked him up next day. He was fine. She took him home and he looked quite normal. There certainly wasn't any bruising. When she got him out of his cot the following day after that though, he had massive bruising at the side of his face so she took him to hospital and they wouldn't allow me to see him. Then they x-rayed Anthony and decided that his ribs were broken and that I must have squeezed him for this to happen but I didn't. They didn't arrest me for weeks after that either. Strangely, the x-rays have been examined by different radiographers and they cannot agree on which ribs they think are broken.'

'How did Jenna get from one side of London to the other side when she picked Anthony back up', Carly asked, 'Does she drive?'

Lawrence shook his head.' Jenna doesn't drive, she travelled back on a number of buses.'

'She would have hardly have done that if Anthony's face had been covered in bruising would she?' Carly remarked thoughtfully. 'People are always wanting to coo over new born babies.'

June 1991

The next meeting with the head teacher and various others from the different organisations was even more bruising than Carly had normally found them. The head teacher was of the opinion that Lawrence should be moved from Carly's care. It was her opinion that Lawrence needed to live in a two parent family and have a dad that he could play football with and take him places.

'I play football with him and I take him places!' Carly asserted.

When Lawrence came home from school the following day, he asked Carly to stop the head teacher from taking him into the office. She was insisting that he tell the social workers that he wanted to go somewhere else where he could have a dad and be taken out places.

'I want to stay here,' he informed Carly. His bright enquiring eyes had fixed themselves on Carly. 'I like it here.'

Carly rang the social worker up. The social worker just thought it was the ramblings of a disturbed little boy but Carly did not think so. Lawrence would not have wanted another dad other than Paul Smith and further, Lawrence was quoting words that the head teacher had voiced in the meeting. A meeting to which Lawrence had not been party to.

Carly was frustrated. She knew that Lawrence was telling the truth but she was just a mere foster carer. Her opinions would only ever be taken into consideration if they agreed with the professionals in this case. That's how it was.

Lawrence continued to protest that he wanted to stay in lessons and not be taken out to have to go to the head teacher's office. 'I want to stay in my lessons and learn things!' he had stated in a voice full of desperation.

With some consternation, Carly contacted Lawrence's solicitor who arranged to find a solicitor for Carly. Caroline was a cheerful and confident advocate. She wrote a letter to the local authority asking them to conduct an investigation.

The result of that was that the head teacher had indeed been taking Lawrence out of his lessons and 'counselling' him to say that he didn't want to stay with Carly. What struck Carly was that the head teacher clearly did not think that what she had done was in any way wrong even though Lawrence had been so frightened that he had hidden under the head teacher's desk.

Lawrence was not taken out of lessons again though. The head teacher retired shortly after.

May 2009

Jenna was small and pretty – even prettier than the photos that Lawrence had sent Carly. Carly put her arm around Jenna.

'When are you two going to get married?' Carly asked them with half a smile on her face.

They both beamed but didn't reply.

'We're going to see Anthony this afternoon,' Lawrence remarked. 'The foster parents have invited us over so that you can see him.'

'We're looking forward to that,' Carly remarked nodding at Mike, 'aren't we, Mike?'

Mike nodded. Normally chatty, he left most of the conversation to Carly, Lawrence and Jenna. After all, Carly was single when Lawrence first entered her life. Mike didn't meet them both for some years after.

The drive there was uneventful. Carly still hated London traffic but was beginning to get used to it. Even as they all walked up to the foster carer's house they could hear Anthony. He was as noisy as Lawrence used to be and that was very noisy.

Anthony was also as energetic as Lawrence used to be, running up and down at top speed and pretending to be an aeroplane. He had a large bruise on his forehead and cheek.

'Where did he get those from?' Carly enquired.

The foster carer smiled. 'That one on his forehead he got when he ran into the table but that one on his cheek. I don't know. He went to bed perfectly fine and the next morning he had this huge bruise on his cheek.'

'Did you take him to the doctors when that happened?' Carly asked.

'Social services don't want us to. They said if we did that they would stop us fostering!'

1993

Lawrence blossomed. He ended his years at infant school passing with the highest grade possible in all the subjects. His six weeks with Carly had turned into over a year. There had been limited visits with members of his maternal side but they were not regular. Lawrence had a change of social worker and was attending a family centre where staff were amazed that he could recall visiting when he was just a toddler. 'Where's that red car which used to be park over in that corner?' he had asked much to their astonishment.

The meetings began to increase. The local authority felt that a decision had to be made about Lawrence's future. While Paul Smith visited regularly, he did not want Lawrence to live with him. Really, there was no place for Lawrence to go.

'Why can't I adopt him?' Carly had enquired. 'He's been with me for a long time and he's settled in well and is blossoming'

The social worker laughed.' You can't adopt him. Lawrence is black and you are white.'

'You wanted to send him back to his birth mother and she is white.'

The social worker ignored this and scribbled something on a piece of paper. 'We will arrange for Lawrence to be adopted through the Thomas Coram foundation. That's final. I'll start this process off now.'

May 1991

Carly, Jenna and Mike returned to Jenna's flat. Carly was touched by how Jenna had tried to make her and Mike as comfortable as possible. The garden was only match box size. Carly thought of the wide open spaces for children to run around in, back home, and quietly grieved.

She did not say much. Jenna and Lawrence were clearly loving and bewildered parents. Jenna explained that she'd had high blood pressure –pre-eclampsia - and Anthony was born by caesarean with forceps. He'd been a little early – about a couple of weeks - and was to all intents and purposes a healthy and lively baby.

'Was there any bruising on Anthony's ribs to suggest that anybody could have squeezed him?' Carly asked.

'None!' replied Jenna. 'None at all. We don't understand any of this. We have solicitors though. Maybe they will help us.'

'Who's paying for them?'

'Social services pay for them.'

Carly wondered how Jenna could be so innocent.

'You and Lawrence will need to make a Subject Access Request for all your files to do with any dealings with the local authority. I think you will find them very revealing.'

'We didn't do anything,' Jenna protested, shaking her head in bewilderment. 'We love Anthony. We just want him back!'

Carly didn't say anything. She didn't think it would be that simple but she didn't want to alarm Jenna.

Tomorrow she would be travelling back home but she was sure that she would be back in London very shortly. Yes, she was sure of it.

Late 1993

'We haven't been able to find Lawrence two black parents yet. They are in short supply so the local authority was looking at a single black parent for Lawrence.'

'And have they found a parent for Lawrence?' Carly asked the social worker.

The social worker shook her head. 'No, they haven't so we tried to find a two parent white family.'

'And?'

'We couldn't find a two parent white family.'

'That leaves a single white person.'

The social worker nodded briefly.

'Why can't I adopt him?' Carly asked. He's been with me now for well over a year and he has come along very well. No-one else has managed that. He'd been in and out of foster homes before he came to me.'

'We wouldn't allow you to adopt him?'

Carly was frankly puzzled. Her mind went blank. Just for once she wished that she could think quickly on her feet instead of being the reflective thinker that she was.'

'We'd probably let you long term foster him though.'

'But he needs the surety of having a permanent home. You said he needed an adoption placement so why are you prepared to let me foster Lawrence long term but not allow me to adopt him?'

'I have to go now,' the social worker said. She stood up and stroked her skirt. 'I have a theory. I think the brains of the working class are all in their pants.' She picked up her case and move silently towards the door leaving Carly aghast at what she had just heard.

The guardian ad litem visited the next day. 'When Lawrence is finally placed for adoption, are you happy for him to continue visiting the Smiths?'

Carly nodded. 'The more people that love a child, the better,' she remarked.

The guardian jotted that down. 'Thank you, he said, 'I need to lay this in the court.'

Early June 2009

The piles of documents which had been delivered to Carly's home at the request of Anthony and Jenna was revealing. Jenna's documents which would be laid before the court were mainly centred around medical records during and after her pregnancy. There was a few hundred pages of documentation of heavy medical information. It did not phase Carly. She had wanted to take up medicine before illness had stopped that in its tracks.

The documents also revealed that a male social worker had already been up to peruse Lawrence's records. Apparently, he had made a weird selection of the documents. It appeared that Lawrence had presented to the consultant paediatrician with whip marks on his back. There was one document which stated that the birth mother had said,' Lawrence caused those himself.'

A second document contained the consultant's remarks which said that it was impossible that Lawrence could have caused those whip marks on his back.

Carly found out later that the social worker only took back the document which contained the birth mother's remarks. This document was eventually used by the forensic psychiatrist as evidence that Lawrence was deeply disturbed as he had self-harmed.

Carly could only think that anyone who selectively used information in that way was the disturbed person and there appeared to be a lot of disturbed people involved with Lawrence and Jenna's case.

Further, the forensic psychiatrist, in her one to one sessions with both Jenna and Lawrence had informed them individually that she did not know who had harmed Antony 'but clearly someone had.'

Again, there was clear lack of knowledge of other factors that may have resulted in the alleged deliberate injuries in an otherwise happy, smiling baby

----

Autumn 1993

The two social workers which were stood on Carly's doorstep were not smiling. Indeed, one looked quite thunderous. 'We have come to see you,' the older one said, 'because we have been notified that you have said that you would be happy for Lawrence to continue seeing the Smiths.'

Carly was bewildered by their hostility. 'Yes, Lawrence loves Paul and he has visited regularly. He has been a stabilising factor in Lawrence's life.'

'We forbid it! If you don't inform the court that you do not agree with Lawrence continuing to see the Smith's, then we will take Lawrence off you.'

'I can't agree with what you are asking,' Carly retorted, 'I can only tell the truth but, of course, you can put forward your opinion to the court, if it is different.'

The social workers left but Carly did not think it would be the last that she heard from them. In fact, she was quite sure that it would not be so.

June 2009

Looking through the papers there appeared to be a lot that didn't add up. Anthony had been born a little early. His mother had had pre-eclampsia and Anthony had been born by forceps during a caesarean. Jenna was working indoors during her pregnancy and her diet consisted mainly of beef burgers. She had laughed when she had told Carly that. She had breast fed Anthony, too.

Jenna was also black and most likely to have been vitamin D deficient. As Anthony had been born early then the lines seen on the ribs which had been considered to be fractures were areas of cartilage which hadn't yet turned into bone. They were very common in premature babies or babies who did not have enough vitamin D to make bone. They had a name. They were called 'Looser's Zones.'

Vitamin C deficiency also causes poor synthesis of collagen which, on x-ray, would appear to be fractures, even though they were not.

Carly wondered why, with all the above information at the radiographer's disposal why this hadn't even been considered. It was incongruous that Anthony could have been squeezed so tightly that a number of his ribs had fractured without any bruising or adult finger marks on his body at all. It was very strange – so very strange.

Indeed, if such force had been applied then internal injury would surely have occurred and there was none. Moreover, the baby maintained his happy and lively personality, something that he would not have done had these alleged injuries been deliberate and real.

Carly looked for evidence of testing for vitamin D. The document simply stated that it could not be completed due to insufficient blood being taken.

Further, testing of vitamin C status had not taken place, either.

Carly was annoyed. It was as though everything had been thought of beforehand and the evidence which could have proven Jenna and Lawrence's innocence had simply not been carried out or in the case of the vitamin D test had been abandoned as 'insufficient sample.'

Carly discovered another document which showed that another blood sample for vitamin D had been taken four weeks later. It had come back within normal limits.

Carly rang Jenna up. 'Did you continue breast feeding Anthony once you took him to hospital?'

'No.' replied Jenna, 'He went straight onto formula.'

Carly rang up a medical friend. 'How long would it take to correct a vitamin D deficiency in a baby who was breastfed but then went onto vitamin D enriched formula?'

'Only a short time, Maybe a couple of weeks.'

'Thanks,' said Carly and put the phone down carefully and thoughtfully.

Autumn 1993

It was obvious that Lawrence had been playing football again. His legs were covered in dark patches which mottled his tanned skin. If he had been white, then the bruising would have been much more obvious. He was an active kid though – always on the go.

He was now in a football team, in cubs, in a swimming club. There was nothing that he didn't want to do. He engaged wholly with life. His smile and enthusiasm was infectious and……… and ………… Carly had grown to love him.

While Carly went into visit Caroline, Lawrence amused himself in the waiting room. She could trust him with that. He would be happy chatting to the receptionist. He was a sociable little boy.

Carly explained the dilemma to Caroline. 'I don't just want to foster him long term. I want to adopt him so that he has the surety of knowing that he can never be moved again but the local authority won't allow it.'

Caroline leaned forward smiling. 'How long have you been fostering Lawrence for?'

'Well over a year,' Carly replied.

'Well, you don't need the local authority's permission then,' Caroline responded. 'you can make your own application once you have fostered a child for a year.'

The application papers were filled in before Carly left the room. She had a feeling that it would not go down well with social services and, as it happened, she was not wrong.

Late June 2009

Carly did not enjoy the second trip down to London any more that she had enjoyed the first. She had already gathered lots of information which cast doubt on the reasons for arrest. Too many things did not fit together.

Lawrence wanted Carly to meet the social worker and his solicitor. Carly wasn't sure about either. People had nasty habits of twisting things to suit their own purposes. She had discovered that in the past. Still, could it harm? Perhaps she would meet them and let them know what a lovely boy Lawrence had blossomed into – finally - when he had finally been cut free from all the professionals in his life who made decisions without any thought of the impact of these on a little boy's life.

Really, she could only tell them how well he had done at school, that he had been a key player in the local football team, that he had passed some GCSE's at the age of fourteen and had been in scouting for all the time that he had been with her.

'Why do you think Anthony's ribs were fractured?' the social worker asked Carly.

'I don't think they were. I think that Jenna was vitamin D deficient throughout her pregnancy and her breast milk was vitamin d deficient. The baby was born early and the lines on his ribs would have been incomplete ossification of the bones.'

The social worker wrote it all down. Carly asked that she sign it.

None of this reached the report that the social worker finally wrote up for the court. When Carly asked to see the original copy she was told that it had been destroyed.

Apparently, this was allowed. It could be destroyed when it was no longer needed.

Early winter 1993

The social workers were spitting furious when the information came from the court that Carly had applied to adopt Lawrence. Firstly, though, they had a request from the birth mother to see Lawrence. They had set the meeting up for the following day, for after school. Lawrence would go to the book fayre with his birth mother and the social worker.

Carly dressed Lawrence in his best clothes. She was thankful that she had only just bought him some new clothing. She'd had to, Lawrence was growing rapidly. It was only 5am; Lawrence had always been an early riser but she didn't mind. She was an early riser too.

Lawrence liked his T shirts. Some old grandad style vests had been sent with his clothing originally and he had refused to wear them. Carly could see why. Lawrence liked dressing up. He was already quite fashion conscious.

Carly wasn't sure how the visit would pan out. The birth mother had taken a dislike to Carly and had made a number of complaints about her. None of them had stuck but that did not mean that they had not made Carly feel any the less anxious.

Strangely, the social worker had also said that when she had made a recent visit to Lawrence that he had seemed neglected. This infuriated Carly since the social worker had not been around for many months. She asked for the date when this supposed visit had taken place. No-one responded.

Carly placed a complaint in with the Local Government Ombudsman who obtained a date. The social worker could not have seen Lawrence at his home on that date. On the date given, Lawrence, Carly and her youngest birth son were 70 miles away enjoying the camp that they had gone on for that week.

The fact that she had complained to the Ombudsman did not go down well with social services.

Prior to the trial July 2009

The trial had been set for the July. Two weeks had been set aside for it. There was to be a bruising expert and a couple of radiographers. Surely, anybody would be able to see that a child could not be squeezed so hard that their ribs broke without any bruising evident on their torso.

Carly wished there had been an expert on nutrition who could confirm that Jenna was most likely to be vitamin D deficient and that the lines were Looser's zones. These often fooled experts into believing that there was a real fracture.

Carly had even found a researcher, who had undertaken a great of research on allegedly battered babies who actually had not been battered at all. He had acted as an expert witness on a number of occasions. He had been hounded out of the medical profession eventually for his views.

Carly found plenty more examples of babies who had been taken off their parents and been adopted before an underlying medical condition had revealed the reason for the baby's signs and symptoms. These were good loving parents who had had their baby snatched cruelly away from them.

It seemed there was little investigation into why some injuries had resulted. It was automatically accepted that it must be the parents. No alternative was sought by the authorities and even for solicitors representing the accused, due diligence appeared half hearted.

The trial was not far away now. Carly and Mike travelled down to see Lawrence again.

Lawrence had found his birth grandmother. It was the search for his paternal birth family that had set Lawrence on his adventure to London. They called in to see Anthony. He was sporting another bruise on his cheek – again this one had just appeared. 'Take a picture of it, Jenna,' urged Carly.

They went to see Lawrence's grandmother who was a petite black lady – a former midwife. During the afternoon, she pointed to a painting on the wall. 'I was brought up by white missionaries,' she said, 'my mother died in childbirth.'

'What did she die of?' asked Carly, intrigued.

'She bled to death.' came the brief reply.

Carly sat up. 'Does anyone else in the family have bleeding problem or do they bruise?'

The grandmother smiled. 'I bled heavily when I had my period. Lawrence's brother nearly bled to death after a routine circumcision. Bruising? My skin's black, it would never show.'

Lawrence was mixed race as was Jenna. Anthony was very light skinned. The bruising showed on them alright. Lawrence had always had bruises even when there did not appear to have been any injury beforehand.

December 1993

The birth mother did indeed put a complaint in. She and the social worker had decided at the last minute that they would not go to the book fayre but would take Lawrence swimming instead. The birth mother just happened to have some swimming gear for Lawrence with her. It did not sound like a last minute change of mind. It sounded very much planned to Carly. When the birth mother had undressed Lawrence she had produced a soot stained vest which she showed to the social worker. She said that she had pulled it off Lawrence. She cited this as evidence that Carly was neglecting Lawrence and should not be allowed to adopt him.

Carly had smiled wryly when she heard this. She had returned all the vests to the social worker some time ago since Lawrence refused to wear them. It had even been entered in the file that this had been done. Carly knew that she would have to record and log everything now.

There was something not quite right about what was going on. There hadn't been for a long time but she had just found it difficult to believe. This was the stuff of fantasy novels. Sometimes she felt as though she was in Alice in Wonderland.

The next day when she was walking Anthony down to the shops he had a massive nose bleed. It wasn't the first that he'd had. They just came from nowhere and wouldn't stop. They dripped down his new T shirt. Carly only had a plastic carrier bag with her to try and mop up the blood. She pinched the top of Lawrence's nose and still it would not stem the flow of blood.

Carly took Lawrence to see the nurse, the following day, at the surgery.

'Ach! The nurse remarked, 'He'll have been picking his nose, that's all.'

Carly knew that that wasn't the case.

However, the consultation was ended at that point.

Carly rang the number for the haematology department. She was hesitant describing the symptoms that the grandmother had, her son and Lawrence.

'Oh! That's Von Willebrand's,' the disembodied voice said.

'What's that?' Carly asked with some relief and some shock in her voice.

She was given an explanation but the words were a jumble going round and round in her head. Why had nobody realised this? Why had no-one tested Anthony for this and why had she allowed herself to be dismissed so readily when she had taken Lawrence to see the nurse.

The hospital promised to send her some information on Von Willebrand's. Meanwhile, Carly looked it up on one of the medical websites. It said:

Von Willebrand disease
Von Willebrand disease (VWD) is a common inherited condition that can sometimes cause heavy bleeding.

People with VWD have a low level of a substance called von Willebrand factor in their blood, or this substance doesn't work very well.

Von Willebrand factor helps blood cells stick together (clot) when you bleed. If there isn't enough of it or it doesn't work properly, it takes longer for bleeding to stop.

There's currently no cure for VWD, but it doesn't usually cause serious problems and most people with it can live normal, active lives. **Symptoms of von Willebrand disease**

The symptoms of VWD may start at any age. They can range from very mild and barely noticeable to frequent and severe.

The main symptoms are:
- bruising easily or getting large bruises
- frequent or long-lasting nosebleeds
- bleeding gums
- heavy or long-lasting bleeding from cuts
- in women, heavy periods and bleeding during or after labour
- heavy or long-lasting bleeding after a tooth removal or surgery

In some people, there's also a small risk of problems such as bleeding in the gut (causing bleeding from the bottom) and painful bleeds into joints and muscles.

Now Carly understood. She understood everything. She understood why Lawrence had bruised so easily and why his nose bleeds had been spontaneous and dramatic.

Anthony certainly did not have his ribs squeezed until most of them fractured. If he had been squeezed in that way, he would most certainly have bled to death given this condition and he would have certainly had pronounced bruising which had not happened.

Carly rang Lawrence up. 'Tell Jenna to get Anthony tested for Von Willebrand's disease,' she urged her.

Not many days later, Jenna had reported that the GP had refused to have Anthony tested for Von Willebrand's disease.

No reason was given.

Carly knew the family were battling against something but she did not know what. She would have to find a private clinic who would test Anthony for Von Willebrand's. By now she did not trust anyone. There was something strange going on and she didn't know what.

Surely, justice is what everyone was seeking.

It appeared not.

Meanwhile both Jenna and Lawrence had been to see the forensic psychiatrist. She had decided that, as Lawrence had been brought up in care, that he must have psychiatric problems which had caused him to harm Antony.

Carly remarked to Mike, 'If the powers that be believe that placing children for adoption is not going to make the slightest difference to them, why do they do it in the first place?'

August 1994

The adoption went through without a hitch. 'Really,' Carly had remarked later, 'It was the only thing that had gone alright in the strange years since Lawrence had come into her care. Even when Lawrence had been round to see his new junior school, the head teacher, from the infant school who had 'counselled' Lawrence inappropriately had insisted on speaking to the junior school head teacher first.

After this meeting, she had emerged from the office and swept past Carly without saying a word. The new head teacher didn't even introduce herself. She stood in front of Lawrence. 'If you ever dare complain about anyone, I will have you and I'll let the High School know you are coming, too.'

Carly was taken aback; Lawrence once more adopted his guarded look.

During his early months at the junior school, he came home sporting huge bruises where someone had thumped him. Repeated complaints to the school did not result in any action.

Lawrence did join the gymnastics class after school. Carly went along to watch one day. Lawrence was sitting cross-legged on the floor, with his friends, watching some other children somersault. One girl, at the opposite side of the school, got up, walked over to Lawrence and hit him hard across the face.

If Carly had not seen it with her own eyes, she would not have believed it. She made an appointment to see the head teacher the next day but nothing was done to prevent it happening again.

That was the problem, nothing ever got done.

Still, Lawrence bloomed academically. He was streets ahead of his contemporaries in every subject and he was also very physically able. He soaked up everything, even learning how to make his bed, iron and cook simple meals. He was socially adept, too.

After Carly's run in with the local authority they would not allow her to adopt again. Carly often wondered if there were any professional people who behaved like professionals - who could accept that other people had different points of views without sinking to the level that she had witnessed.

Since she was not allowed to foster or adopt anymore, she advertised the spare room to the local university. She specifically stated that she wanted an eighteen-year old female student so she was more than a little surprised when Mike applied.

That's how Carly met him. That's how Carly met her future husband.

It was shortly after that, that Lawrence came home from school. He was particularly concerned that the

Non- Teaching Assistant had pushed a young boy, with learning disabilities, into the table and hurt him.

Carly's heart sank. She knew that Lawrence did not make things up. Indeed, when further investigations had been undertaken into what had been passed off as the 'disturbed mutterings' of a little boy, (his infant school experience with the head teacher) there was no doubt that it was not Lawrence who had been disturbed. That was the hard thing to bear. How can you bring children up in a world where there was so much that was wrong going on?

The following day, Lawrence came home and reported that the same thing had happened again only this time, he had stood up and informed the NTA, who was responsible for pushing the pupil, that she was 'not a very nice person.'

In response, the NTA had tipped the table up so that all the books and pencils had slid off onto the floor.

'I am a nice person!' she thundered until the children cowered back in the seats.

The teacher during all this commotion continued to write on the board as though nothing was happening. It did not surprise Carly – everybody seemed to hide their heads in the sand these days. No-one seemed to have any integrity at all, nowadays. No, not one person.

Carly took Lawrence out of school that day. She sent a letter of complaint to the LEA at the same time informing them that she was deregistering Lawrence from formal education. She would home educate Lawrence since the school were not able to keep up with his academic ability, anyway.

Most of all though, Lawrence would not be safe at that school. She recalled how the gymnastics teacher had seen the girl walk from one side of the hall to the other to hit Lawrence across the face, entirely unprovoked. She had wanted to say that she had misinterpreted what she had seen, but she knew that she had not. The teacher had witnessed the act and had done absolutely nothing about it. Absolutely nothing!

Carly allowed Lawrence to set his own subjects. That was the beauty of home education, you weren't confined to a narrow curriculum.

Lawrence was only eight at the time; he chose to read The Mystery of Edwin Drood and undertake a project on whales to begin with.

He would work through his maths books and learn a few different languages. He would do this by borrowing DVD's from the library. For history, he opted to learn about 'black' history and study people like Martin Luther King and Rosa Parkes. For his first geography project he chose to look at Jamaica. Of course, there would also be cooking and nutrition and visits to faraway places.

Carly was already planning these.

Lawrence was extremely sociable. He was a member of a local football team where he was a prolific goal scorer.

He was a member of the cub scouts where he enjoyed going on all the camps. He went swimming with his best friend, went out with his dad at the weekend and generally sported a huge grin wherever he went.

Carly was at peace although the stress of the years battling with the authorities had left her exhausted. One day when she tried to speak the words would not come out, they were stuck in her head. She made an appointment with the doctor.

Day before the trial July 2009

Carly had one last brief day with Lawrence and Jenna before the trial started. She had taken most of her limited saving and given it to them in case .... In case things did not turn out as they planned. She wanted them to have a good night out – a meal and a movie, maybe.

They were young, naïve even. Neither of them could contemplate other than a return of not guilty for they were, indeed, not guilty. They were confident that the court would see this. They had good barristers, so they thought, and had every confidence in them.

Carly had looked through the papers again – all the documents that the young couple had that would be laid before the court. The forensic psychiatrist's report did not resemble anything about the young couple which Carly knew to be true.

How was it that someone could make a decision about somebody else's life that might impact on them for the rest of their lives, when they had only seen them for a few hours?

'I have to go,' Carly whispered to the couple. 'I have other responsibilities at home. You both have people who can support you though, don't you?'

They both nodded vigorously and smiled broadly. Carly turned and stepped into the car where Mike was waiting. When she turned back, Lawrence's demeanour had dropped. He looked very young and vulnerable and she regretted that she had responsibilities and could not stay.

September 1994

The GP stated that he would send Carly to a neurologist. There wasn't a local one at the time so she would have to travel out to a different area. Carly wasn't all that bothered. Her pre-adoption medical had been fine so it would just be over tiredness. It wasn't surprising; it had been a long battle.

Meanwhile there was Lawrence to attend to. He had now read a number of the works of Shakespeare and some more of Charles Dickens. He was learning some Mandarin and a little Latin. He had covered more than the maths he needed to do for the year.

Carly had taken up teaching privately. This meant she could be at home for Lawrence and still make an income. She was one of the few private tutors who would tutor children with special needs. She had a lovely young boy, Chris, who came with his Mum, for tuition. He had mild learning needs but he was a quiet, well behaved and polite young man.

Chris's Mum was quite agitated one day. Chris was a lovely year old that Carly was teaching privately. He had reported to his mother, that the NTA had pushed him into the table for no reason at all. He was genuinely upset. Mrs Law wanted to take it up with the school but, 'Who would believe a child?' she asked in consternation.

When Carly questioned Mrs Law, it became clear that it was the same NTA who had threatened Lawrence and who Lawrence had witnessed pushing another child with special needs into the table.

'I was glad that I placed in a formal complaint,' she later told Mike, 'otherwise there would have been no record of what had taken place and it would have been much more difficult for Mrs Law to prove what Chris had said.

The following week when Mrs Law arrived with Chris she was informed that the NTA had taken early retirement.

It was some time before Carly was informed that she had multiple sclerosis although she had already guessed this.

The consultant had spent a lot of time stroking Carly's foot with a bunch of keys and looking puzzled. Carly could see that she had Babinski's sign which meant that something neurological was going on. She shrugged. It never rained but it poured.

'I think we need to get Lawrence into school,' she remarked later to Mike. 'He's not going to the local high school. The head already informed me that she would inform the school when he was coming.' That wasn't just making conversation, that was a threat!

Lawrence was already streets ahead of his contemporaries. He had been tested by a psychologist who the solicitor had found prior to him being adopted. He was found to be perfectly normal and sociable and further in the top 2% of the world population for intelligence.

This did not surprise anyone who knew Lawrence.

Still, he was not of high school age. This did not stop Carly looking around for grammar schools. Perhaps he could take the entrance exam a year early. Eventually, one was identified. The head teacher interviewed Lawrence and was satisfied Lawrence could cope, provided he passed the exam. Then, of course, there would be the matter of fees.

Carly was shocked. Fees? Would Lawrence not get an assisted place?

The head teacher leaned forward. The assisted places were for those boys of high school age and Lawrence was a year younger.

Carly pursed her lips. First of all, Lawrence had to take the exam. He did and passed with flying colours. Mike found a charity who specifically helped children who had been in care. A lady came and interviewed Lawrence and was happy to offer him the fees for the first year.

They all went out that night and celebrated.

It was a good day when Lawrence started his first day at school. Carly could breathe properly again. It was the first time for a long while that she had been able to do so.

Almost immediately there were problems. Lawrence came home saying that he had been spat on when he was on the school bus and that racist remarks had been made. Someone had burnt him with a cigarette.

Carly asked Lawrence to sit at the front of the bus but it didn't make any difference. She could feel her heart sink. Lawrence was only one of two black boys at the school. Naively, she had believed that the school would stamp out any form of discrimination. She was wrong.

Carly asked to see the head teacher who blamed the cigarette burning, the racist remarks and spitting on Lawrence even though he was the very youngest child there.

Carly, once again, thought that she was living in a world run along the lines of that found in Alice in Wonderland.

Still, at the end of the first year 1996, Lawrence was placed third out of 120 boys and he was the youngest, by a year at least, of all the boys.

The six weeks' summer holidays gave them all some respite. Carly was hopeful that things would settle down by the time Lawrence returned to school. She was wrong.

Shortly, after the first term of his second year, Lawrence came home with a huge round bruise on his leg and a significant tiny circular bullseye in the middle of it. Lawrence stated that he had been shot with something. Carly could see that Lawrence wasn't lying. He *had* been shot at with something.

With a sinking heart, Carly informed the school who insisted that Lawrence had made it up although the injury was evidence that he had been shot at with something.

Carly was now convinced that nobody was interested in Lawrence's welfare. It was as though there was an unseen malicious thread warping Lawrence's future. She had not come across racism before. She had been brought up to have honesty and integrity and to ignore what was going on would be as much as abusing Lawrence as had happened to him before he had arrived at her house all those years ago.

Carly put her complaint in writing. There was still a small part – albeit a very small part – that wanted to believe that someone actually wanted to put Lawrence's welfare first.

In response, the school, removed Lawrence from the classroom and asked his classmates to write down what they thought of Lawrence. These were shown to Carly. Strangely, all of them said exactly the same thing. They all said that Lawrence was a bully and they were frightened of him. This didn't make sense. Lawrence was a sociable little boy and very popular in his groups at home. He was also the youngest in his class. He was hardly intimidating.

Two notes were missing. They were produced later when legal papers crossed hands. They said that Lawrence was a good friend and fun to be with. It later transpired that some parents had remonstrated with the school for its heavy handedness with Lawrence.

Carly was pleased that at least two young lads would grow up to have some integrity. They had refused to write notes which had clearly been dictated to them.

The school said they could no longer accommodate Lawrence. 'Find him another school,' they said. 'We will write him a reference.

Carly knew that Lawrence was no longer safe at the school so she deregistered him and began looking for other another school for Lawrence. This took a long time. When she had found one she found that the assisted place was not transferable and she could not afford the fees.

Mike and Carly set about home educating Lawrence who thankfully, settled back into home study, easily. He gained his maths GCSE at the age of fourteen and a number of other GCSE's at the age of fifteen, one or two years earlier than he would have been expected to have taken them.

Just as things had begun to settle down, Lawrence reported that a man named Sid would appear from near the graveyard, when Lawrence was on the way to scouts, and ask him if he wanted to find his birth dad. Lawrence had always wanted to know who his birth dad was and did not seem in the slightest bit fazed by this unknown person accosting him.

Carly was not at all happy with this. Of course, she wanted to help Lawrence find his birth dad, but not at this moment when he was in the middle of his education. Lawrence didn't need his life messing up, yet again.

The final visit from the Local Education Authority officer came about. Lawrence had plans to undertake some missionary work abroad. He was described as a mature and conscientious young man in the officer's report. Indeed, Lawrence was. He had turned out to be a mature, sociable, hardworking young man.

To supplement his clothing allowance, Lawrence had found himself a paper round. He deposited his earnings in his bank account every week. When he had worked overseas, he wanted to set up his own business but he was also hoping to be taken on as a professional footballer. Until……. Until……. . that day that changed his whole life.

Lawrence had not seen his birth mother from very shortly after his adoption. She had simply not taken up contact which had been provided for her by the courts. She had been Paul Smith's cohabitee but, as far as Carly knew, they did not see each other or have contact with each other after Lawrence had been adopted.

Paul Smith had a son by another woman. That suggested that the relationship had been over for a long time.

Carly did not know that both Paul and Lawrence's birth mother worked together in the night clubs. She was more concerned about Sid who turned up frequently when Lawrence was walking through the village. He was like a shadow. He seemed to know when Lawrence would be strolling on the High Street. It wasn't as though he had done anything wrong. He simply asked Lawrence if he would like to meet his birth dad. It wasn't a criminal offence.

Lawrence, anyway was fifteen now. Even if Carly reported this Sid, it was clear that Lawrence was happy to stop and chat with Sid. His wishes, at his age, would override any concerns that Carly had about the wisdom of unsettling the child at this important stage in his academic life. Lawrence was very determined to know who his birth father was.

Lawrence hadn't been a difficult teenager to bring up. You would have thought he would be considering his difficult early start. He was very mature – much more mature than his contemporaries – in many respects. Of course, he had his moments but they were not as long or as profound as some of her friends were experiencing with their children.

'Lawrence!' Carly shouted up the stairs, can you finish the English assignment off? It has to go no later than tonight's post!'

'OK, Mum!' was the cheerful reply.

That had been the stressful bit, helping Lawrence organise all the assignments to be marked by an external examiner. It wasn't cheap. No, home educating a child wasn't cheap at all.

There had been more outside groups for Lawrence to join so that he wasn't missing out on his social education and development. Then there were all the academic books.

Of course, some could be obtained from the library but generally not for long periods.

Registering with external examiners had cost a great deal and the postage to send Lawrence's assignments to the examiner – all by recorded post – wasn't cheap either. She would be glad when this last lot was safely in the post. The post office closed at half past five and it was now nearly four pm.

There was a knock at the door. An irate neighbour was reporting that Lawrence was flying paper aeroplanes out of his bedroom window and they were landing in his garden.

Carly looked at him in disbelief before apologising profusely and making her way upstairs. Lawrence was indeed flying paper aeroplanes out of the window.

'What are you doing?' Carly asked in disbelief. 'You're supposed to be getting your assignments together. They have to be posted tonight at the latest. Please get your things together now. You're grounded for this evening.'

Another knock at the door alerted her to the fact that her pupil had arrived. Carly hovered between wanting to speak further with Lawrence and the need to greet her pupil. She trusted Lawrence to get on with things and besides, she needed to work to pay the bills. She alerted Mike to the fact that Lawrence was packing the assignments and could he post them as soon as he had.

Carly was agitated throughout the lesson but she kept her calm. She had prepared the lesson, for her private pupil, well beforehand and so it did not need a great deal of delivering. She was half way through the lesson when someone else knocked on the door.

This time it was Paul Smith.

Carly stared at him blankly. He hadn't rung to say that he was taking Lawrence out but he muttered something along the lines that he was taking Lawrence out for a beef burger. Lawrence shot down the stairs when he heard Paul's voice.

Mike had already made his way up to the post office.

'I've grounded him.' Carly explained.

Paul stood impassively, waiting. His ways were different. They always had been but they had managed to work alongside each other for Lawrence's sake.

Carly didn't have time to explain. Her pupil was waiting and he was paying for an hour's tuition and every minute she was standing here was time that was taken away from that hour.

'I'll speak to you later,' Carly said. 'Take Lawrence now. I've got a pupil. I'll have finished in less than an hour.'

Paul turned up at 8.30pm.

'Look,' Carly said.' I need you to understand that I would like you to contact me first to see if it is OK for Lawrence to go out. He was grounded and he's been rewarded by being taken out for a beef burger.'

Paul Smith did not want to discuss things. He was – and always had been – a man of few words. 'I'll keep Lawrence overnight until the heats died down.'

Carly was weary. It had been a long day. 'Go one then,' she said. Even then she thought to herself that she would rue the day that she said that.'

That day come soon enough.

The telephone rang the following day. It was 11am and the day was already warm and sunny. Carly picked it up and waited for Lawrence to speak only……. it wasn't Lawrence.

'This is Judy Jones from social services. I'm just ringing to let you know that Lawrence is back with his birth mum.'

Carly was stunned. Her brain was trying to process what had just been said. 'Birth mother? No, he's just stopped overnight with a gentleman who he classes as his dad. He's coming back this morning – I thought it was Lawrence that was ringing.'

The disembodied voice on the end of the telephone sounded bewildered. 'I'm sure I was told it was Lawrence's birth mum. I'll go and check and get back to you.'

When the officer rang later, it was clear that Lawrence had been taken back to his birth mother's.

Carly sat and thought long and hard about this. Clearly, this had been planned for a while but by whom, primarily? She couldn't hire a solicitor, she had barely anything in the bank. Further, she'd had enough dealings with the birth mother in the past to know that it could be a long, drawn out vindictive affair. This had already impacted on Carly's health. She had to think of herself and Mike now.

Lawrence was fifteen now. He was tall and strong and quite able to deal with any physical abuse that dared to be meted out to him. Carly had to let him go and hope the years that she'd had with Lawrence were enough to give him the skills he needed to weather any storm that he came across.

That was the last that she heard from Lawrence until the letter came some years later.

She had seen Paul Smith in the town though, sitting in his truck with his elbow stuck of the window in his usual fashion.

He was bitter. Hollow. Lawrence had apparently gone to London looking for his birth father soon after he had been deposited at his birth mother's house. This had wounded Paul Smith beyond measure. 'Somebody should have disciplined that lad.' He muttered angrily.

'That's what I was trying to do,' Carly reminded him.

He looked and didn't say a word. She left. At the bottom of the street she turned to wave. He didn't notice; he looked deep in thought.

She didn't see Paul again. He died two weeks later. He had a heart attack and didn't recover.

Three days into the trial, it was clear that things were not going well for the couple who each had different barristers. Lawrence would ring up and inform Carly of the main points. 'Why didn't the barrister mention this? It was valid,' she remarked angrily.

On the fourth day, Lawrence remarked, 'My barrister says she could do with you coming down here.'

'I'm on my way,' Carly said. She roused Mike from his nap, threw some clothes into a carrier bag and set off for London yet again. The courtroom had been emptied by the time she arrived but outside courtroom three were masses of people who seemed to be supporters of Lawrence. Carly eventually found out that they were most of the paternal side of Lawrence's family. He had many half-brothers' but there were also friends.

Carly met Lawrence's grandma. She kept muttering that she could not understand why a certain type of forceps were used when Antony was born The marks could still be clearly seen on Antony's forehead where the pressure had been applied.

They were the wrong ones. The hospital had used the wrong ones. She wanted to give evidence to this effect but wasn't allowed as she was family.

Carly recalled that Anthony had quite pronounced marks on the side of his face which had been caused by the forceps. It appeared from the birth records that Anthony had had quite a difficult birth.

Carly did manage to see the barrister before the next session. Carly did not know what to make of her but did manage to correct some of the evidence which had been given. She mentioned that Lawrence most likely had Von Willebrand's and had passed it onto Anthony.

'Could they please get Anthony tested as social services did not want him to be and he had already spontaneously bruised in the care of the foster carer's?' she asked in desperation.

The judge denied them this request. They'd had plenty of time before the trial to do this, she had stated.

Carly was not allowed to explain that she had only just discovered the family history and put this information before haematology in a local hospital.

In fact, she wasn't allowed to explain anything and all the while the jurors sat there. They did not need to listen to the evidence. They had already made up their minds before they came to court. It was written all over their faces. Yes, it was.

Their faces were impassive ………. Stern … save for a couple who thought the whole thing was a joke and giggled and passed notes frequently between each other. It was a farce.

The expert witnesses were called. One was a bruising expert.

'In the event of a bleeding disorder,' she said. 'I cannot explain the bruise on the child's face.'

Carly was screaming inwardly, 'but there is evidence, there is! Why won't anyone have Anthony tested for Von Willebrand's?' Why aren't the foster carers observations allowed to be put forward in evidence?

The radiographers were just as convinced about their diagnosis. They likened the 'rib fractures' to being those seen in a high speed car crash. No-one mentioned that the two independent reports could not even agree on which ribs were affected. No-one mentioned that for such 'squeezing' to have occurred that there would have been considerable bruising on the torso and there was none. Indeed, such alleged compression would have produced internal injuries and there were none.

Carly knew, by now and with a more or less 100% certainty of Von Willebrand's that there would have been severe and potentially fatal bruising on Anthony's body if he had been squeezed hard enough to cause rib fractures; and there had been none. None at all apart from that on his face which hadn't been there when Anthony had left Lawrence's or even for three days after that.

But, it seemed no-one wanted to listen and all the time Lawrence sat in the witness box being accused of hurting his son. The son, it was clear, he loved dearly.

Lawrence had taken blows all his life and had survived them but the one thing he could not cope with was being accused of hurting his son.

The day before the trial ended, Carly had to return home. There was no more money if she didn't work. She kissed Lawrence and hugged him hard. She kissed Jenna and hugged her hard. She did not promise that everything would be OK. She was not sure that it would be, ever again, for any of them.

The Epilogue

Lawrence and Jenna were both convicted of harming their son. Jenna was directed to have psychiatric input but Anthony was returned to her. Lawrence was given an Indefinite Prison Period (IPP) for three years but eventually ended up serving seven years because he refused to admit to something that he hadn't done.

Even after seven years he refused to admit to harming Antony. The evidence had never been there, tests hadn't been carried out, Antony's bruising did not manifest itself until 3 days after Lawrence last saw him. The baby was still engaged and happy.

Significantly, Antony was bruising spontaneously when in the care of the foster parents where he had been placed for some weeks.

Lawrence was imprisoned for seven years having been given an Indefinite Prison Period.

Lawrence was released after still maintaining his innocence.

The psychiatric report produced at Lawrence's trial stated that he had a personality disorder. On release he was tested again and found not have a personality disorder.

This after seven years of being threatened on a daily basis by other prisoners and having no clear idea of when, if ever, he would be released.

When Anthony was returned to Jenna, Carly paid for Anthony to have the blood test undertaken privately as the GP refused to do it. The blood test did show that Anthony had Von Willebrand's which causes extensive and spontaneous bruising, without injury.

Carly wrote to the prison and asked that Lawrence be tested. This took months and then, apparently the wrong colour test tube was used so it was abandoned and the whole process had to be gone over again.

When Lawrence did finally have the blood tests it caused extensive bruising the whole way down his arm. Although this was evidence of a bleeding disorder, Lawrence still needed the results of the blood tests - which nearly took a year to obtain - given the mistakes in using the wrongly labelled test tube.

Nevertheless, when the results finally came through, Lawrence was also found to have Von Willebrand's which made a good deal of sense about his childhood.

I think there were two injustices here. I take you back to Paul Smith who was accused of abusing Lawrence. He vehemently denied doing so, when Lawrence was taken into care, and consistently stayed with that stance.

There is no doubt that Paul Smith and Lawrence had a good relationship. It was inconceivable on watching them first time around that there was anything but a deep bond between them. Yet I recall, the social worker involved, making discriminatory comments about Paul Smith because he was 'obese.' Indeed, this was written in the social worker's notes.

The association made was that as Paul Smith was obese that he must have been the one who abused Lawrence and caused the bruising.

While the birth mother was found to have abused Lawrence, this took the form of horse whipping for which he had scars on his back.

The bruising – and the nose bleeds – had entirely different causes from that of the whip marks and, if it had been caused by some form of physical punishment could not have occurred due to whipping.

There are so many failures in information gathering, even at this point, that it is unbelievable; concerning is that most of them appeared to be deliberate. Even when Carly took Lawrence to see the nurse for what were prolonged and dramatic nose bleeds the only response was that it was due to Lawrence 'picking his nose.'

The radiographers could not agree on which ribs were 'fractured.'

No account was taken of the fact that there were no internal injuries, no fingerprint or hand shaped bruising on the child or that the child was otherwise happy and well; something which, you may agree, the baby would not be if the bruises and alleged fractured ribs were due to actual physical injury.

The Judge: HHJ Louise Kamill

The judge who was sitting in the case above, was allowed, in another case, to take an important document home, and did not forward it to the criminal court of appeal as they should have done. On 6th January 2013, a reader 'Lotus' remarked about this case that:

When members of the public are criminally convicted, fined and sentenced without any basis in law, the law being invented, fictitious and not in British law or any other law on this planet, it seems that appeals are denied and the appeal forms vanish and judges steal them for bedtime reading for a laugh.'

Carly did contact Lawrence's solicitor with the news that Anthony had Von Willebrand's as this would have been useful for the appeal but the solicitor never responded.

Lawrence's relationship with Jenna no longer exists. He only sees his son on an occasional basis and it is unlikely Lawrence will reach his academic potential given that most of his time had to be spent trying to prove his innocence. He has approached various legal firms to see if they can get his conviction quashed in the light of his and Anthony's diagnosed bleeding disorder.

All of them have replied that it is too complex a case.

Justice has not been done.

The same Judge, HHJ Louise Kamil, sitting at Snaresbrook Crown Court, has had another conviction quashed at Curt of Appeal: "the failure to make sure that counsel was aware of both the fact and content of jury notes was a material irregularity...rendering the convictions unsafe"

Case No: 201900005 C1/

/ 20190015 C1 / 20190017 C1

In the court of Appeal (criminal Division) on appeal from Snaresbrook crown Court

HHJ Kamill

Royal Courts of Justice

Strand, London, WC2A 2LL

1/12/2019

In a separate case HHJ Kamil imposed a sentence that 'was only explicable on the basis that it enabled the sentence to be suspended.'

'We are satisfied that the judge failed to give sufficient weight to the inherent seriousness of this type of offending.'

CASE NO 202002746/A2

IN THE COURT OF APPEAL

CRIMINAL DIVISION

Royal Courts of Justice

Strand

London

WC2A 2LL

Given the behaviour of the judge in Lawrence's case and subsequent failures that have come to light, a robust investigation is needed into cases which she has been involved in and which span at least two decades.

HHJ Kamil's refusal to allow Antony to be tested for Von Willebrand's disease is damming. No one had looked at the family medical history. Indeed, Lawrence as a fostered – and eventually adopted child – had known nothing of his paternal side. Further, even the grandmother did not have a name for the bleeding disorder that appeared to run in the family. It had never been linked with any named condition nor even considered that it might be responsible for Antony's bruising.

It was only when knowledge of Lawrence's vulnerability to nose bleeds and bruising was added to that of Antony's, and a family history taken, did it begin to make any sense.

Any judge interested in real justice, who had not already made their mind up as to the outcome of the case, would have adjourned the trial until both Lawrence and Antony had been tested for a bleeding disorder. After all, the medical 'expert' on bruising and bleeding had stated that, 'in the absence of a bleeding disorder, I cannot explain the bruising.'

However, Antony had not been tested for a bleeding disorder but the court bypassed that as though it were of no consequence.

Other potential risk factors for spontaneous bruising and similar manifestations found in 'Shaken Baby Syndrome'.

Von Willebrand's disease is not as rare as the medical books would like you to believe. Lawrence would probably never have been diagnosed if he had not passed the condition onto Antony. His susceptibility to bruise would have been explained away by his active lifestyle. His heavy nosebleeds due to 'picking his nose' although this had never been the case.

How easy it is for medics to explain away something because their knowledge is incomplete. All it would have taken though is for the nurse who turned Lawrence away to ring up haematology 'just in case.' Better than that 7 years of imprisonment for an innocent life.

But..... what of those accused of Shaken Baby Syndrome who perhaps do not have conditions like Von Willebrands? Are there other potential causes that have not yet been explored along with the failure to investigate nutrient deficiencies as potential causes of alleged injury.

In the majority of cases that I have come across, the criteria for finding guilt 'beyond all reasonable doubt' has not been met. There appears to have been little motivation for looking beyond the assumption that such injuries could only ever be due to systemic abuse by one or both parents.

Such assumptions have denied innocent parents the joy of bringing up their children, of making a home, of living in private for everything is taken off them and all, regardless of whether it is a true version of events, or not, is laid bare.

The higher criteria of beyond all reasonable doubt compared to that of the civil 'on the balance of probabilities' was meant to prevent the conviction of innocent people but it depends on the quality of evidence and clearly the expert witnesses are not as expert as they believe themselves to be.

They are experts in a very narrow field and the danger is that facts may be chopped and shaped to fit an expert's expertise.

Who chooses these experts? The people who choose them are non-experts with only a belief that such a person that they have picked will be able to respond in the direction that they wish the trial to take.

Do they, at any time in the future, come across evidence that causes them to take a sharp intake of breath as they realise that what they genuinely thought to be the truth, is not and that they have played a huge part in sending an innocent life to prison?

A number of research papers that were written in the early 2000's has not reached the exposure that they should have. Why this was, is not the subject of this book although many may reflect upon it. Indeed, given all that has been revealed so far, it should be a matter of conscience that further robust enquiry should be made if we would like to believe that we are seekers of truth.

Two of these papers looked at the impact of vaccines.

They are discussed in more detail below. What you may discover may well surprise you.

Two Pertinent Research Papers

At the time of the events written about two important research papers had already been published. One, a review by the highly respected BMJ Review of Hear the

Silence,[1] has remained largely unheard of. Given the huge importance it has for health across the ages but also for considering an alternative reason for Shaken Baby Syndrome, it begs the question why this knowledge has not been used in preventing side effects in those who wish to take vaccines. It is reproduced in its entirety below.

Review of *Hear the Silence*
BMJ 2004; 328 doi: https://doi.org/10.1136/bmj.328.7430.51 (Published 01 January 2004)Cite this as: BMJ 2004;328:51

Rapid Response:
The prevention of vaccine reactions

We know that reports of severe reactions following infant vaccinations, though rare, are causing widespread anxiety among the population. Moreover, physicians are discussing the question as to how many days after vaccination an infant death should be considered as attributable to a vaccine (1).

---

[1] https://www.bmj.com/rapid-response/2011/10/30/prevention-vaccine-reactions?s=03

A review of the World literature on vitamin C and vaccine reactions in animals has revealed that supplementary vitamin C (ascorbic acid) has a potent and highly significant protective effect (2).

Ascorbic acid reduces both the morbidity and the mortality following the injection of all bacterial and viral toxins tested in guinea pigs, and even in rats and mice, which make their own ascorbic acid from simple sugars in the liver.

Clearly, even the ascorbic acid-producing animals do not always make enough ascorbic acid for all their needs. The highly protective effect of vitamin C has also been reported in children by Kalokerinos (3) in his studies of aborigines in Australia.

One therefore cannot help wondering why the various national centres for disease control have not yet recommended vitamin C to be given before all vaccinations. It would surely be most beneficial, not only in reducing severe vaccine reactions and deaths, but also in reducing or preventing the residual disabilities which can occur following minor cerebral or subdural haemorrhages.

We now know that the bleeding of severe vitamin C deficiency (or scurvy) is due to capillary fragility arising from the accumulation of excessive levels of histamine in the blood (4), causing widening and separation of the tight-junctions between the endothelial cells of the capillaries and venules, from which the bleeding arises (5).

The histamine accumulation in scurvy is due to the fact that ascorbic acid is essential for the body's progressive removal of histamine by converting it to hydantoin-5-acetic-acid and on to aspartic acid in vivo (6).

Nowadays, with so many vaccines being given simultaneously to infants, one has to consider that the histamine arising from the injection of these foreign proteins and the histamine arising from any childhood infection will be added to the already elevated blood histamine level due to ascorbic acid depletion, so leading to a toxic blood histamine level which can be fatal.

Perhaps this severe condition should not be called Infantile Scurvy or Barlow's Disease, but rather Toxic Histaminaemia or a Barlow's Disease Variant.

No doubt Health Departments will soon conduct studies of plasma, ascorbic acid and whole blood histamine levels on soldiers before and at various intervals after single and multiple vaccinations for overseas duty. Such studies will certainly confirm that outwardly normal people with somewhat low ascorbate levels have markedly elevated blood histamine
levels, and that their blood histamine concentrations

increase even more
following vaccinations.

A more useful estimation of the time range of vulnerability for each vaccine might then be made.

Until then, we can hope:

1) That vaccinations will be postponed when an infant is premature or is ailing in any way, even with the common cold.

2) That consideration will be given to reducing the number of vaccines to be given at one time.

3) That 500 mg of vitamin C powder in fruit juice will be given to
infants to drink before their vaccinations. (More vitamin C can be given by intramuscular injection, if the infant develops a high-pitched cry, a febrile illness, or has a convulsion.)

Additionally, I would recommend that if the above measures are not undertaken then there is no proof that the criteria of 'beyond reasonable doubt' has been met.

There was little - taking all the above into consideration - that could convict anyone of Shaken Baby Syndrome on the evidence that was produced at Lawrence's trial.

I would further suggest that unless vitamin D and C sufficiency is tested for immediately a child is found to be suffering from alleged Shaken Baby Syndrome, then this raises a huge question over any assertion that the parents – or other caregivers – have harmed their child.

My opinion is that temporary 'brittle bone disease' does occur as it has the ability to do so in some form or another throughout anyone's life.

Sometimes, we call this osteopenia or osteoporosis but this fragility of bone occurs due to nutritional deficiency whether it is in the form of vitamin D, vitamin C, magnesium or countless other nutrients which are required for optimum health of the complex structure known as bone.

We live in the age of fast food which has little nutritional value. Even though we are encouraged to eat '5 a day' or in some cases '10 a day' the underlying assumption that we will all ingest more than enough vitamin C for our needs is false.

The recommended daily intake for vitamin C currently stands at 75mg for women and 90mg for adult males but are we being lulled into a false sense of security when it comes to believing we have eaten our vitamin C requirements for the day?

We are taught than a medium sized orange contains about 30mg of vitamin C. However, is that when it is plucked straight from the tree or after it has travelled half way around the world, been placed in a supermarket, bought then placed in a fruit bowl before it is eaten.

Vitamin C dissipates rapidly in storage.

Even local vegetables suffer a similar fate. Light and heat dispense with vitamin C quickly. Cooking eliminates about 95% of vitamin C. That mean that you are probably taking in so little that suboptimal scurvy is present.

Only, we don't recognise it because we are not a third world country so how can a nation as great as ours, as wealthy as ours have conditions of nutritional deficiency?

This is the current thinking? Is it born of ignorance or hype which seeks to convince people that they have never had it so good when they are being fed with 'food' with the nutritional content of cardboard?

Very few people grow their own food where they can pick it fresh from the garden and have it on the plate within half an hour. That was a 1950's way of living which is found in very few households now.

Vitamin C deficiency is easily able to cause severe bruising. Skin and blood vessels become fragile without vitamin C. Collagen is also needed for proper synthesis of these, not just bone. Fragile blood vessels bleed often spontaneously or with just the slightest knock.

In elderly, we often see a 'bleed in the brain' causing stroke but does anyone wonder about the underlying cause?

What happened to a young healthy individual to reach the stage of having a bleed into the brain?

The second piece of research,[2] a feature article was entitled Shaken Baby Syndrome or Vaccine-Induced Encephalitis written by Harold E. Buttram in response to the death of Alan Joe Yurko, a baby who died at 10 weeks of age shortly after receiving 6 vaccines. The father was given a life sentence for Shaken Baby Syndrome although many believe that he had been wrongly convicted.

This paper is robust in the amount- and breadth - of information that it imparts but appears to have had little recognition. However, it contains vital information and challenges the assumptions of most expert witnesses that only violence by a significant other could have caused the injuries that have brought the defendants before the court.

---

[2] Buttram H. Shaken baby syndrome, or vaccine-induced encephalitis? Med Sentinel 2001; 6:83-89.

Using the research found in this paper, which is worth seeking out, I wrote a blog surrounding some of the issues that it contained.

Vaccine induced encephalitis - a blog

The above mentioned research papers from **2001** and 2004 highlight the oft hidden dangers of vaccines. The first written by Harold E. Buttram, MD was originally published in the Medical Sentinel 2001; 6(3):3-9. *Copyright @2001 Association of American Physicians and Surgeons* investigates the diverse negative impact of vaccines and asks, 'Are the symptoms of Shaken Baby Syndrome actually Vaccine- Induced Encephalitis?

The Second paper   Review of *Hear the Silence* was published in the respected BMJ on January 1st 2004; 328:51. It poses the question, 'When vaccine reactions can be avoided by given a nutritional supplement why hasn't this been undertaken?'

Shaken Baby Syndrome (SBS) was very much in the news in the early 2000's. John Hemingway MP was looking into the increase of cases at the time but it's not clear whether this affected the outcome of any of the cases that came before the court. However, although it reached prominence —enough for an MP to investigate - the concept of SBS had been mooted in the 1970's with a number of explanations – none of which had evidence to back them up – being offered to support the hypothesis.

Radiologists, haematology experts, paediatricians and psychiatrists could not proffer an alternative viewpoint for the injuries said to be due to Shaken Baby Syndrome yet the evidence for another cause had been raised loudly and clearly and yet had oddly been silenced by the media.

Medical opinion that bleeding from subdural haematomas requires new trauma, is disputed. Whenever trauma has occurred, such as trauma suffered during birth, new bridging veins may rupture as the subdural haematoma expands. This has nothing to do with injury.

Retinal haemorrhages are assumed to be the result of non-accidental head trauma yet it is well known that there are many other causes such as repeated coughing during an asthma attack or respiratory infection. There is a diversity of causes which also include the MMR and DTP vaccines.

The pertussis vaccine is used to induce allergic encephalomyelitis in laboratory animals. Symptoms include brain swelling and haemorrhage, indistinguishable from deliberate injury such as that found in SBS.

Dr Archivides Kalokerinos noted that deaths following vaccination in poorly nourished children were virtually eliminated once vitamin C levels were restored.

Histamine sensitivity has been found to be a characteristic of day 4 and day 12 of from the pertussis vaccine.

Rib fractures are not directly related to vaccines but loss of vitamin C due to vaccines could cause incomplete collagen synthesis forming areas which result in spontaneous fractures. Areas of incomplete collagen synthesis may also resemble fractures. Where rib fractures exist, which are due to genuine deliberate traumas, these injuries were also accompanied by severe internal thoracic injuries.

Dr Kalokerinos quoted, *Scurvy disrupts these areas, the bone breaks down, and the ribs may override, forming in typical cases 'beads.' Then healing commences with new bone formation looking like true healing fractures. Furthermore, not all the ribs may be involved in this process, and the changes will not all occur at the same time ----- giving the appearance of multiple fractures of different ages*

Further, this type of fracture is found in scurvy and does not need any form of trauma to manifest itself.

In 1955, electroencephalograms were given to 3 children before and after the pertussis immunisation.

Two children, who had previously normal results prior to the EEG were found to have abnormal scans after. Buttram poses the question whether the minimal brain dysfunction that ensued was the reason for the attention deficit hyperactivity disorder (ADHD).

It is important to realise that vitamin C deficiency (scurvy) results in capillary fragility due to unopposed histamine levels. Vitamin C is well known for reducing the amount of histamine produced and is an excellent natural antihistamine. Without sufficient vitamin C the removal of histamine via its conversion to hydantoin-5-acetic acid and from there onwards to aspartic acid cannot occur. If the child is already vitamin C insufficient and the histamine cannot be removed the impact can be devastating. Histamine continues to increase and if unopposed may result in death.

Bear in mind that if a virus or other infection is brewing then vitamin C levels will be depleted even further.

The practice of giving numerous injections at the same time appears to be an unwise one. No one knows if the child is about to manifest an infection which has already reduced the amount of vitamin C available. No one checks for the status of vitamin C in the child prior to injections being given and shockingly the BMJ's recommendations have been ignored.

When there is a large body of evidence showing that vaccines have diverse negative effects - especially in the presence of vitamin C deficiency - and the medical profession fail to respond to this, then it is a parents' duty to take that responsibility upon themselves and demand that vaccines, if they are required, be given singly. Further, 500mg of vitamin C should be given prior to any injection given.

This may well prevent a lifetime of disability or, at worse, death.

-

I add this further paper:

Doctor accused of misrepresenting evidence in child abuse cases

I had the privilege of talking to Dr Colin Paterson, who is the subject of the headlines above, on a number of occasions. At the time I was involved in the case which is the subject of this book. As a medical nutritionist, I was aware that incomplete ossification of bones would occur in prematurity and in nutritional deficiency.

Antony was premature. His mother had high blood pressure during late pregnancy and the birth had to be induced. Forceps had to be used, too. This is all vital information which cannot be discounted in the quest for truth and how they may have resulted in the injuries that Antony had.

While my interest and research was focussed on vitamin D at the time, vitamin C deficiency (scurvy) can also cause peculiar abnormalities in bone due to poor synthesis of collagen.

Collagen of course is the main protein in connective tissue such as bone.

I would remind you that the first blood sample for vitamin D had to be abandoned due to 'insufficient' vitamin D. Antony then was placed on formula and a blood test for vitamin D deficiency taken nearly a month later.

When I enquired of the medic (although I already knew the answer) as to how long it would be before any deficiency would be corrected, I was informed 'two weeks.'

It seems strange that an insufficient sample was taken after which the baby was given nutritionally rich formula milk and some time passed before another sample was taken for vitamin D deficiency. At this point any deficiency that had existed, would have been corrected.

I agree with Dr Paterson's expert opinion and do not publish it here with any other than that in mind.

BMJ. 2004 Jan 24; 328(7433): 187.

doi: 10.1136/bmj.328.7433.187-a

PMCID: PMC1140657

PMID: 14739179

Doctor accused of misrepresenting evidence in child abuse cases

Owen Dyer

Copyright and License information PMC Disclaimer

A Scottish chemical pathologist is facing charges before the General Medical Council of misrepresenting medical evidence as an expert defence witness in child abuse cases. Dr Colin Paterson frequently testified that seemingly non-accidental injuries were actually caused by temporary brittle bone disease—a condition that he himself first described and whose existence is disputed by many experts.

Dr Betty Spivack, an American expert in the biomechanics of abusive child injury, giving evidence to the GMC via a video link, said that temporary brittle bone disease was not "a recognised disease" or "generally accepted condition," "I wish he would come up with the evidence to convince people like me who think that it is a lot of rubbish," she said. "He does not have the experience and training in this field."

On three occasions, British judges criticised Dr Paterson's evidence. On the last of these occasions, in the High Court care case in March 2001 of a young girl referred to only as X, Mr Justice Singer accused him of "tunnel vision," saying his evidence was "woeful."

Following that incident Dame Elizabeth Butler-Sloss, president of the Family Division of the English High Court, complained about Dr Paterson to the GMC. The GMC sent him a formal letter notifying him of the complaint.

Three months later, Dr Paterson travelled to Arizona to testify in the retrial of Audra and Martin Talmadge, who had appealed against convictions for injuring their daughter Amber. The retrial was granted partly because Dr Paterson had not been allowed to testify in the original trial.

The GMC's charges relate to the "child X" and Talmadge cases. In the child X case, Dr Paterson is accused of ignoring bruises suggestive of traumatic injury.

In the Talmadge case, he is accused of not adequately studying the documents in the case, of misrepresenting the views of other doctors to suggest they agreed with his views on temporary brittle bone disease, and of adapting the indications of the disease to suit the symptoms shown by the child. The charges say he discounted vomiting as evidence of the disease in the child X case, but included it in the Talmadge case.

Dr Paterson, now retired and formerly a reader at Dundee University, first proposed a condition he called temporary brittle bone disease in the Journal of the *Royal Society of Medicine* (1990;83:73-4). He described it as a self-limiting osteogenesis imperfecta with spontaneous improvement, and with numerous fractures confined to the first year of life.

Over the following years, by his own estimation, 60 to 70 children were returned to their parents in cases where he testified.

The GMC case began in November (*BMJ* 2003; 327:1124) but was adjourned over the Christmas period. It is expected to finish next week.

In the Talmadge case it appears that nothing other than the accepted narrative will do. Why can there not be a temporary condition? Throughout pregnancy, mothers are given iron tablets and folic acid so that they and their unborns will be healthy.

Magnesium deficiency is a known cause of the very high blood pressure that often complicates the end of a pregnancy.

Vitamin D deficiency is rife and vitamin C deficiency is apparently the fourth most common nutrient deficiency in the US.

However, I have never come across any Shaken Baby Syndrome case where nutrient deficiency has ever been considered, something I also find very strange.

I believe all the pieces that need to be revealed to deliver a very different verdict to that imposed upon Lawrence, have been placed before you.

Here was an innocent young man, who was subject to ignorance, discrimination and a lack of due diligence. These were powerful forces which still are in evidence. They operate without conscience, destroying lives and appear unstoppable.

It is my hope that this case history will go a little way towards being a part of the change that is needed.

A further update on Lawrence and Antony

Shortly after Lawrence was released from prison, he had to spend some time in a half-way house in order to start the adjustment that needed to be made after 7 years in prison.

Lawrence was keen to start building up a relationship with Antony but the relationship between Jenna and Antony had become strained during his long incarceration. This was not helped by interference from social workers who informed Jenna that if she continued to see Lawrence in prison that they may have to remove Antony from her care.

Lawrence was allowed to see Antony provided there was a chaperone. Lawrence had a number of good friends who were convinced of his innocence who were happy to oblige. Still, it was not the easiest way to build up a long overdue relationship when his every action was being observed.

Eventually, Lawrence was able to see Antony alone but many of the meetings that Lawrence tried to set up were sabotaged by Jenna.

It was difficult finding work. After all Lawrence did not have a seven year working history. He had attempted to take a French degree during his imprisonment but eventually the tutor who had been allocated to him from the university stopped going to see him.

Eventually, after a series of menial jobs, he secured a job in IT. It was well paid, with opportunities for advancement. He excelled at the job. Eight years after his conviction, he had entered the world of work he never thought he would participate in any meaningful way, again.

During this time, Lawrence met someone who had not met him prior to the conviction. The relationship blossomed and they made a decision but not before Lawrence's second son was conceived.

After his birth, Carly received a photograph of Lawrence's new born son who was the perfect image of Lawrence at that age.

There was talk of social workers keeping an eye on the family in the early days; someone had informed social services of the impending birth. However, this did not happen although it caused a great deal of consternation for Lawrence and his partner at the time.

With the arrival of the new baby, Lawrence's happiness was complete but we should not forget the years of injustice he suffered at the hands of faceless 'experts' who lacked the professional knowledge to be able to consider an alternative reason for what happened.

Lawrence was, and is, resilient but I wonder about the others. Those parents who did not have the support or upbringing that Lawrence had; those who were not able to fight their case.

Carly had visited Lawrence in prison a number of times and was struck by how many of the inmates had no one to visit them. No one to love them, no one to care. It seemed at times that the most let down by society were to be found there.

We cannot forget the cruelty of the Indeterminate Prison Period (IPP).

An article dated 24th July 2023 stated that indeterminate sentences could amount to psychological torture.

Time to reform "torturous and unfair" indeterminate sentences

Monday, 24 July 2023

Indeterminate sentences across the UK could amount to psychological torture and require urgent reform, argues our latest briefing, out today.

The briefing, *A death row of sorts*, takes its title from the remark of a prisoner in Scotland, subject to an indeterminate sentence.

Life sentence-like indeterminate prison sentences across the UK

All three of the UK's three main criminal justice jurisdictions – England and Wales, Scotland, and Northern Ireland – operate life sentence-like indeterminate prison sentences. Unlike the conventional life sentence prison sentence, which can only be imposed for a relatively narrow range of offences (such as murder), these life sentence-like indeterminate sentences can be imposed for a far wider range of offences.

In England and Wales, the Imprisonment for Public Protection

(IPP) sentence, abolished in 2012 for any new sentences (but not retrospectively) was recently described as "irredeemably flawed" by the House of Commons Justice Committee. The Committee called for far-reaching reform, including a resentencing exercise for all those still subject to an IPP sentence.

In Scotland, the Order for Lifelong Restriction (OLR) combines an indeterminate period of imprisonment, after which the prisoner can apply for release. If granted, they are subject to lifelong restriction on their movements and liberties.

In Northern Ireland, the Indeterminate Custodial Sentence (ICS) operates in a similar way to the OLR and the IPP. The Northern Ireland Court of Appeal has described the ICS as "the most draconic sentence the court can impose apart from a discretionary life sentence".

Unlike the partially-abolished IPP in England and Wales, both the OLR and ICS remain available to the courts in Scotland and Northern Ireland.

Is it torture?

A report last year by the Centre for Crime and Justice Studies highlighted the psychological impact of the IPP sentence on prisoners. Today's briefing asks if the IPP, OLR and ICS sentences could amount to psychological torture. As the briefing points out, prisoners under these sentences face many hurdles, many false dawns, in seeking their release. As a result:

it is the cumulative experience of disappointments and rejections over long periods that is likely to lead to despair and a sense of helplessness. It quotes the conclusions of the UN Special Rapporteur on torture, who argued in 2020 that:

in order to be 'lawful', sanctions cannot be open-ended, indefinite or grossly excessive to their purpose, but must be clearly defined, circumscribed and proportionate

Take action

Earlier this month, the Chair of the House of Commons Justice Committee, Sir Robert Neill, tabled [an amendment to the Victims and Prisoners Bill](), currently making its way through parliament, to allow for a resentencing exercise in relation to those still subject to the IPP sentence.

If brought into law, the amendment would give a definite end date to all existing IPP sentences, and has the support of IPP campaign groups such as the United Group for Reform of IPP (UNGRIPP) and IPP Committee in Action.

I think we have reached the end of our exploration of alternative causes for injuries associated with Shaken Baby Syndrome and the injustices which abound.

It is for you, the reader, to consider the evidence and ask yourself if you would have reached the same verdict as that of the jury?

What elements of the case cast doubt on a guilty verdict being delivered?

Why did the authorities inform the foster carers that if they took Antony to the GP for investigations into his spontaneous bruising, they would prevent them from fostering in future?

So many unanswered questions …….

Other books by this author include:

- The EDS and Hypermobility Syndrome Diet
- Alleviating Symptoms of EDS
- Gastroparesis
- The EDS recipe book
- The Lipoedema Diet
- The Lymphoedema Diet: reverse and repair lymphatic damage
- The Anti Virus Diet
- The Asthma Diet
- The Reluctant Bowel
- The MND Diet
- Why we live longer with higher cholesterol levels
- A dietary connection for MACS, POTS and EDS
- Identity: a self-exploration workbook *
- Journey Through Pneumonia
- https://www.amazon.co.uk/dp/B07TBHMV6N

*This book can be used alone or in small group work and is an excellent resource for those who are 'people helpers.'

Among many others

They are available on Amazon

Lynne has written a semi-autobiographical trilogy.

For the full range of books by this author, visit the author website on

https://www.amazon.co.uk/-/e/B07BPQZ5CD

https://www.amazon.com/-/e/B07BPQZ5CD

A percentage of the profits from the sale of these books go to support charities like the Exodus Project below.

The Exodus Project

My first introduction to the far reaching impact of The Exodus Project occurred when I was travelling around Cawthorne in one of their buses, visiting gardens. A young lad was happily munching on a sandwich. He looked up briefly, pointed to the driver and said,' He's my second dad, he is,' then he returned to his sandwich without further comment

Such remarks are often very telling and so I arranged to meet Jackie Peel and Martin Sawdon, at the charity's premises in Barnsley. They set up the Exodus Project 20 years ago. They moved into their current premises – a redundant Methodist church - in 2010.

Both Jackie and Martin have been youth workers in their church. Martin worked in housing for the homeless in addition to working in learning disabilities services in institutional settings.

The work that the Exodus Project undertakes is of paramount importance to the communities it serves. These were former mining communities which became disadvantaged after pit-closures. Currently about 400 children attend mid-week activities from Monday to Thursday inclusive. These activities include dance, drama, craft, music, sports and games. In addition, there are weekend camps, cycle treks, outward bound activities, bowling and swimming. The children are taught valuable life skills including how to cook and bake. It is all about teaching children how to fulfil their potential and learn skills they will be able to pass onto the next generation.

The grounds, once overgrown, have been turned into a play- and camping - ground. A miniature railway is in the process of being installed.

Martin and Jackie have developed a unique model in that The Exodus Project goes beyond dispensing services. They are keen to build up relationships with the whole family and not just the child that attends the mid- week clubs. In addition, once children have reached the age of fourteen, they are invited to help out with the younger groups as junior volunteers. Once they reach the age of eighteen, they become adult volunteers. This model provides a constant supply of help from individuals who have benefitted already from attending such groups.

The building is large and inviting. It is decorated with bold colours and has comfy seating. It is a real home from home; a haven for families who have been disadvantaged by the closure of the life force of its community.

Martin and Jackie have clear ideas about how they wish to develop the Exodus Project but the lottery funding which they benefitted from is no longer available. Sadly, they have had to close two of their clubs due to lack of funding. This decision wasn't taken lightly. They do have two charity shops which raises some money and they obtain some funding from outside organisations for the use of their facilities. However, this is clearly not enough to keep their clubs, weekend activities and building going to cater for the ever growing number of children who are benefitting from the work being

undertaken here.   Neither does it allow for future development.

Exodus do have a Just Giving page which can be found here if you wish to help further their work https://www.justgiving.com/exodus

In addition, you can keep up with activities on their Facebook page here

https://www.facebook.com/search/top/?q=the%20exodus%20project%20barnsley&epa=SEARCH_BOX

www.ingramcontent.com/pod-product-compliance
Lightning Source LLC
Chambersburg PA
CBHW050308230526
45471CB00005B/2085